Exploring Food Chains and Food Webs

DESERT FOOD CHAINS

Katie Kawa

New York

Published in 2015 by The Rosen Publishing Group, Inc.
29 East 21st Street, New York, NY 10010

First Edition

Editor: Katie Kawa
Book Design: Reann Nye

Photo Credits: Cover Jay Ondreicka/Shutterstock.com; p. 5 (desert) Doug MacLeod/Shutterstock.com; pp. 5, 21 (cactus) Jerry Horbert/Shutterstock.com; pp. 5, 21 (grasshopper) bikeriderlondon/Shutterstock.com; pp. 5, 21 (deer mouse) Stuart Wilson/Science Source/Getty Images; p. 7 Ken Wolter/Shutterstock.com; pp. 8, 21 (kangaroo rat) Brian L. Hendricks/Shutterstock.com; p. 9 emattil/Shutterstock.com; p. 11 Sumikophoto/Shutterstock.com; pp. 12, 21 (mule deer) Don Fink/Shutterstock.com; pp. 13, 21 (jackrabbit) Martha Marks/Shutterstock.com; pp. 14, 21 (rattlesnake) Gordon Wiltsie/National Geographic/Getty Images; pp. 14, 21 (scorpion) defpicture/Shutterstock.com; pp. 15, 21 (elf owl) Rolf Nussbaumer/Getty Images; pp. 16, 21 (coyote) iceprotector/Shutterstock.com; p. 17 Karen Grigoryan/Shutterstock.com; pp. 18, 21 (bacteria) clearviewstock/Shutterstock.com; p. 19 John Cancalosi/Photolibrary/Getty Images; p. 21 (fungi) Martin Fowler/Shutterstock.com; p. 21 (desert) JeniFoto/Shutterstock.com; p. 21 (grass) Smileus/Shutterstock.com; p. 22 Johnny Adolphson/Shutterstock.com.

Library of Congress Cataloging-in-Publication Data

Kawa, Katie, author.
Desert food chains / Katie Kawa.
pages cm. — (Exploring food chains and food webs)
Includes bibliographical references and index.
ISBN 978-1-4994-0093-9 (pbk.)
ISBN 978-1-4994-0095-3 (6 pack)
ISBN 978-1-4994-0090-8 (library binding)
1. Desert ecology—Juvenile literature. 2. Food chains (Ecology)—Juvenile literature. I. Title.
QH541.5.D4K39 2015
577.54—dc23

2014035479

Manufactured in the United States of America

CPSIA Compliance Information: Batch #CW15PK: For Further Information contact Rosen Publishing, New York, New York at 1-800-237-9932

CONTENTS

TIME TO EAT!

All living things get **energy** from food. Some living things make their own food, and some eat other living things. A food chain is a way of showing how energy is passed on when one living thing eats another. A food web shows how different food chains in a **habitat** are connected.

A desert is one habitat that's home to many food chains. The plants and animals in a desert depend on each other for the energy they need to live and grow. Only certain plants and animals can survive in this hot and dry habitat.

Food Chain Fact

All food chains, including desert food chains, start with energy from the sun.

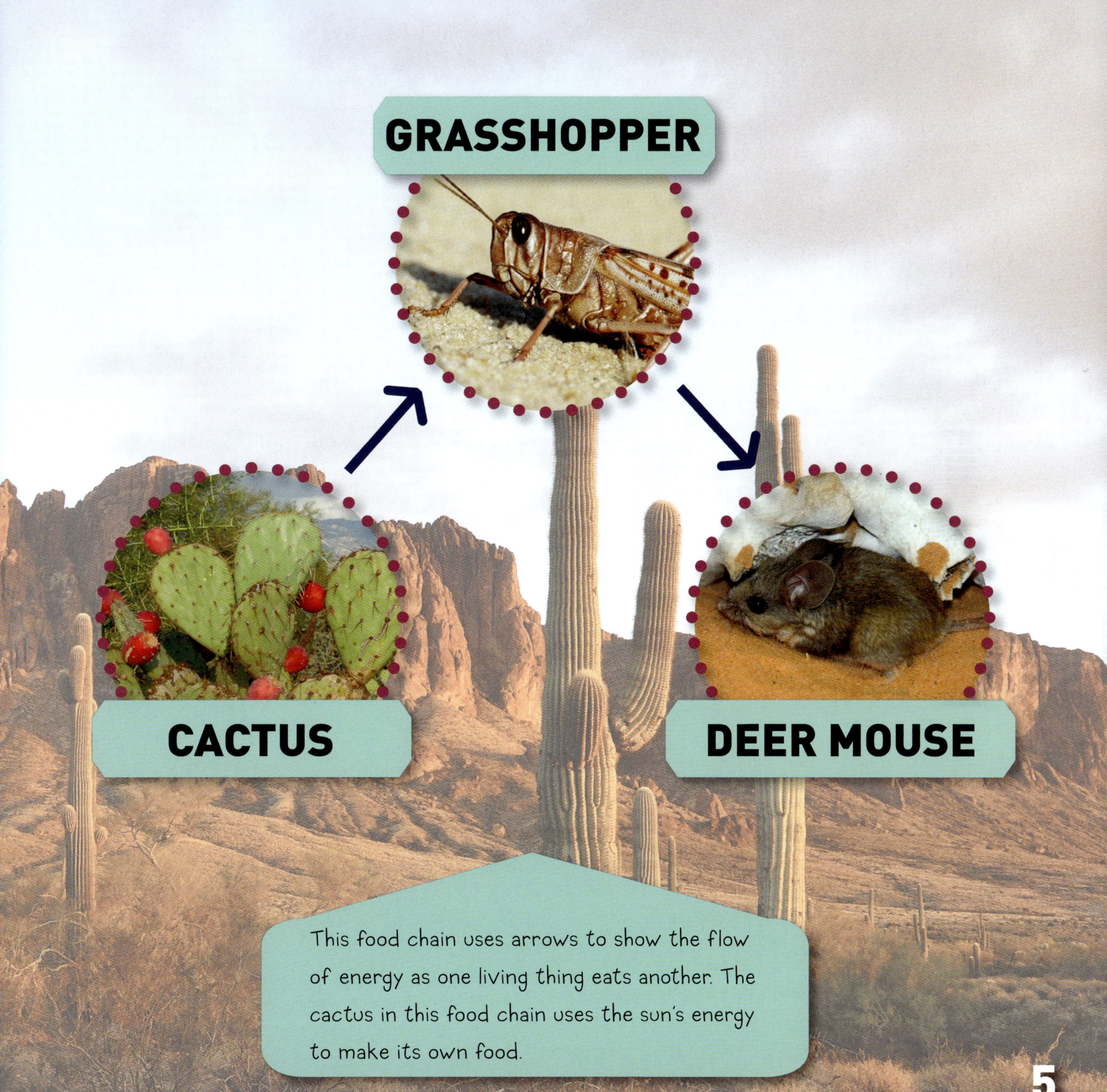

This food chain uses arrows to show the flow of energy as one living thing eats another. The cactus in this food chain uses the sun's energy to make its own food.

LIFE IN THE DESERT

What do you picture when you think of a desert? Do you think of rocks and sand? Do you imagine dust and thorny plants? Do you see the hot sun beating down on the dry land? These are all parts of a desert habitat. However, a desert habitat is not as empty as you might think. In fact, it's home to all kinds of **unique** plants and animals.

Desert plants have special **adaptations** to help them live in a hot habitat with dry soil. Desert animals also have adaptations to live in such an **extreme** place.

Many desert plants, such as cacti, don't have leaves. This is an adaptation meant to help them save water. Plants often lose water through their leaves.

Food Chain Fact

Many desert plants store water in their stems because the soil is too dry for them to get enough water through their roots.

FINDING WATER

Even though deserts are dry habitats, the plants and animals that live in them still need water to survive. Deserts only get a small amount of rain each year. When it does rain, the hot sun causes much of the water to quickly go back into the air. This is called evaporation.

Desert plants and animals have many adaptations that help them get water. The ocotillo has leaves that only appear when it rains. The kangaroo rat gets all the water it needs from the seeds it eats.

Food Chain Fact

The kangaroo rat only looks for food at night because it's too hot during the day. Animals that are active at night are called nocturnal animals. Many desert animals are nocturnal.

The ocotillo's leaves only appear when they're needed to catch rainwater. These leaves make it easier for the plant to collect as much water as it can.

WHAT'S PHOTOSYNTHESIS?

Plants use energy from the sun to make, or produce, their own food. For this reason, plants are called producers. Plants use the sun's energy to turn water and a gas in the air called carbon dioxide into a kind of sugar. This **process** of producing food is called photosynthesis (foh-toh-SIHN-thuh-suhs). When an animal eats a plant, some of the sun's energy is passed on to that animal through the plant.

There's a lot of sunlight in the desert to help plants make food, but sometimes it's too much. The sun can make the air too hot and dry for certain plants to grow.

Food Chain Fact

The leaves of desert plants are often waxy. This helps prevent the loss of water due to evaporation.

Plants, such as these colorful wildflowers, are the first **link** in a desert food chain.

EATING DESERT PLANTS

Plants are the first link in a desert food chain, and the animals that eat them are the second link. Almost anywhere you see plants in the desert, you'll find signs of animals, too. That's because many desert animals depend on plants for food. Animals that eat only plants are called herbivores.

Jackrabbits are common desert herbivores. They're known to eat large amounts of desert plants, including cacti. Mule deer also eat desert plants, including grasses and bushes. Both jackrabbits and mule deer are known for their large ears.

Food Chain Fact

Jackrabbits are actually a species, or kind, of hare—not a rabbit. Hares are larger than rabbits, with bigger ears and longer back legs.

Jackrabbits and mule deer lose heat through their large ears. This helps them stay cool in the desert.

HUNTING IN THE DESERT

Plants aren't the only things eaten by animals in a desert. Some animals hunt and kill other animals in this habitat, too. Carnivores are animals that eat other animals, and they make up the third link in a desert food chain.

Rattlesnakes and scorpions are desert predators that use **venom** to kill their **prey**. Rattlesnakes eat mice, rats, and other small desert **mammals**.

Scorpions are desert predators that eat bugs as well as some species of snakes and mice. Scorpions are prey for other desert predators, too, including the elf owl. Animals that eat other carnivores are called secondary carnivores. Each one creates another link in the food chain.

Food Chain Fact

Elf owls surprise their prey because they don't make any noise as they fly.

THEY'LL EAT ANYTHING!

Some animals eat the bodies of dead animals. They're called scavengers, and they play an important role in desert food chains. Scavengers keep the energy, **nutrients**, and water in the bodies of dead animals from going to waste.

Coyotes are desert scavengers. They eat the bodies of dead animals, but they also eat many other kinds of food. Because coyotes eat both plants and animals, they're called omnivores. Some of the things coyotes eat include jackrabbits, elf owls, grasshoppers, and grasses. Their ability to eat many kinds of food is important because certain foods can't always be found in the desert.

Food Chain Fact

Coyotes have a unique howling call that can often be heard in the desert at night.

Coyotes are found in many habitats. They can sometimes be seen in small towns and even big cities!

DESERT DECOMPOSERS

Plants need nutrients from the soil to produce their own food. Even dry desert soil has nutrients in it. These nutrients come from the dead plants and animals that are broken down in the soil. Decomposers are living things that break down dead plant and animal matter. This process puts nutrients back into the soil, so new plants can continue to grow.

Decomposers include certain kinds of bacteria and **fungi**. Some special fungi grow on the roots of desert plants. Decomposers are the final link in a food chain.

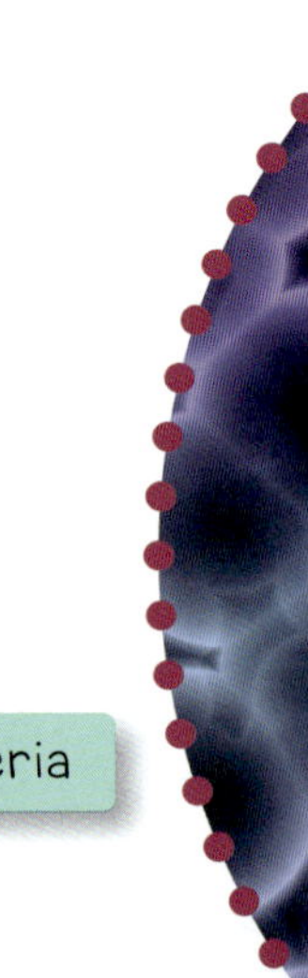

bacteria

Decomposers will help break down the body of this dead cactus, which will put nutrients back into the soil. This will help new cacti grow.

Food Chain Fact

Bacteria are too small to be seen by human eyes.

A DESERT FOOD WEB

All the living things in a desert habitat are connected. This food web shows the connections between several desert food chains.

The colors used on the food web show the different kinds of living things in a desert habitat. The decomposers, shown in gray, break down the bodies of every member of this food web after they die. Follow the arrows to trace the flow of energy from one living thing to another.

Food Chain Fact

A deer mouse is an omnivore because it eats bugs, seeds, and fruit.

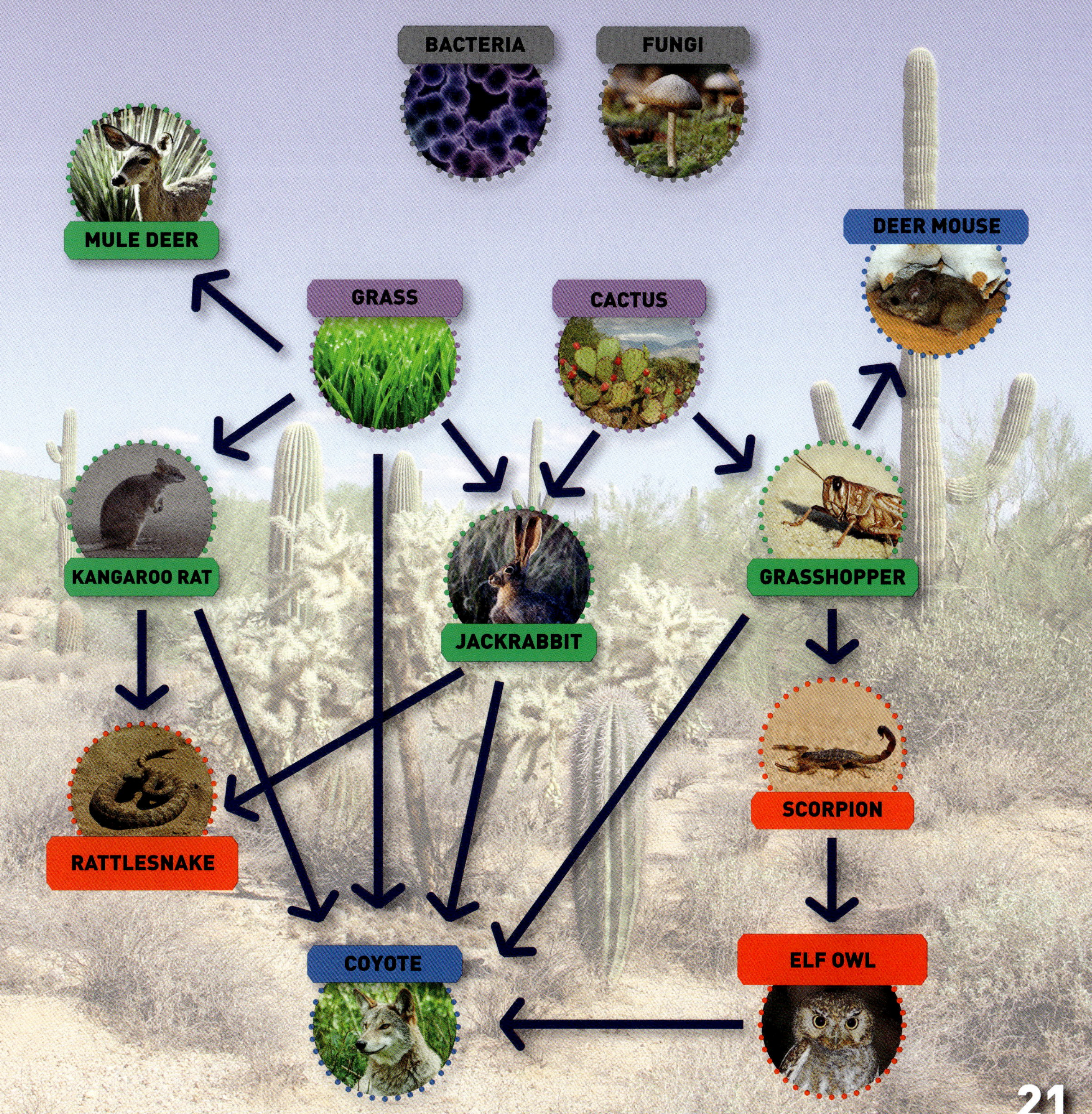
BACTERIA
FUNGI
MULE DEER
DEER MOUSE
GRASS
CACTUS
KANGAROO RAT
GRASSHOPPER
JACKRABBIT
SCORPION
RATTLESNAKE
ELF OWL
COYOTE

FOOD CHAINS IN ACTION

The desert is a great place to visit to see plants and animals unlike any others on Earth. There's more to see in the desert than you could possibly imagine. People have been studying deserts for thousands of years, but new discoveries are made all the time.

It's fun to see how different the desert is during the day and at night. Nocturnal animals make the desert come alive at night, with predators chasing prey and herbivores looking for plants to eat. If you visit the desert, you can see food chains in action all around you!

GLOSSARY

adaptation: A change in a type of living thing that helps it live better in its habitat.

energy: The power or ability to be active.

extreme: Exceeding the ordinary or usual.

fungi: Living things, such as mushrooms and mold, that feed on dead plants and animals.

habitat: The natural home for plants, animals, and other living things.

link: A connecting piece.

mammal: Any warm-blooded animal whose babies drink milk and whose body is covered with hair or fur.

nutrient: Something taken in by a plant or animal that helps it grow and stay healthy.

prey: An animal hunted by other animals for food.

process: A series of actions or changes.

unique: One of a kind.

venom: A poison produced by some animals.

INDEX

WEBSITES

Due to the changing nature of Internet links, PowerKids Press has developed an online list of websites related to the subject of this book. This site is updated regularly. Please use this link to access the list: www.powerkidslinks.com/fcfw/dfc